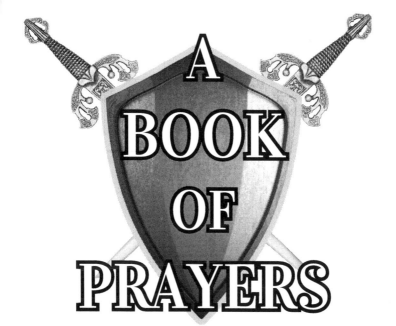

Scripture quotations taken from the Amplified® Bible (AMP),Copyright © 2015 by The Lockman Foundation Used by permission.

Scripture quotations marked (CEV) are from the Contemporary English Version Copyright © 1991, 1992, 1995 by American Bible Society. Used by Permission.

Scripture quotations marked ESV are from the Holy Bible, English Standard Version. Copyright © 2001 by Crossway Bibles, a division of Good News Publishers. Used by permission.

Scripture quotations marked KJV are from the King James Version of the Bible.

Scripture quotations taken from the NEW AMERICAN STANDARD BIBLE®, Copyright © 1960,1962,1963,1968,1971,1972,1973,1975,1977,1995 by The Lockman Foundation. Used by permission.

Scripture quotations are taken from the New King James Version®. Copyright © 1982 by Thomas Nelson. Used by permission. All rights reserved.

Scripture quotations marked NIV are taken from the Holy Bible, New International Version®, NIV®. Copyright © 1973, 1978, 1984, 2011 by Biblica, Inc.® Used by permission. All rights reserved worldwide. New International Version® and NIV® are registered trademarks of Biblica, Inc. Use of either trademark for the offering of goods or services requires the prior written consent of Biblica US, Inc.

Scripture quotations marked NLT are from the Holy Bible, New Living Translation, copyright © 1996, 2004, 2007. Used by permission of Tyndale House Publishers, Inc., Wheaton, IL 60189. All rights reserved.

Scripture quotations marked TLB are from The Living Bible. Copyright © 1971. Used by permission of Tyndale House Publishers, Inc., Wheaton, IL 60189. All rights reserved.

TABLE OF CONTENTS

I	Protection	1
II	Guidance	5
III	Favor	9
IV	Grief	11
V	Health	14
VI	Faith	17
VII	Fear	21
VIII	Family	25
IX	Marriage	30
X	Children	33
XI	Provider	37
XII	Peace	40
XIII	Language	44
XII	Anxiety	47
XIII	Depression	50
XIV	the Father's Prayer	54
XV	Nehemiah's Prayer	56
XVI	Jabez's Prayer	58
XVII	Hannanh's Prayer	60
XVIII	Aaronic Blessing	62
XIX	Jeremian's Deliverance Prayer	64

Protection

Dear Father,

I believe You will keep me as I weather the storms of life. You are my refuge; I ask that You hide me under Your mighty shadow. May your angels take charge over me; no evil shall befall me. Thank You for protecting all that concerned me, my family, my church, and my vision. I desire to rest in the safety of Your wings, knowing that trials do not always last, but Joy comes in the morning.
    In Jesus's name! Amen

Dear Father,

I will rejoice in You, Lord, and in the power of His might. "For we do not wrestle against flesh and blood, but against principalities, against powers, against the rulers of the darkness of this age, against spiritual hosts of wickedness in the heavenly places. Therefore, I take up the whole armor of God, that I may be able to withstand in the evil day, and having done all, to stand "(Ephesians 6:12-13 NKJV). You are Lord, my helper. I will not fear what man does to me (Hebrews 13:6).

In Jesus's name!" Amen.

Dear Father,

I am confident that You are always with me because Your Word says You have began a good work in me, and You will complete it until the day of redemption (Philippians 1:6). Father, I will continue to feed on Your faithfulness. I will be strong and of good courage; I will not fear nor be afraid of them because Your Word says, for the Lord my God, He is the One who goes with me. He will not leave or forsake me (Deuteronomy 31:6 NKJV). Father, thank You for preparing a table before me in the presence of my enemies (Psalms 23:5). Thank You for Your goodness and mercy that will follow me all the days of my life (Psalms 23:6).

In Jesus's name! Amen

Guidance

Dear Father,

As I go through this day, please give me strength and grace in the midst of defeat. I proclaim, You are my Shepherd, and I shall not want (Psalms 23:1). Thank You so much for Your peace and grace as my guide. I trust Your voice and shall follow Your path (Proverbs 3:5-6), for You have ordered my steps. Therefore, no temptation shall overtake or entice me (1 Corinthians 10:13 AMP). Thank You for providing me a way out so I can endure it without yielding and overcome temptation with Joy (1 Corinthians 10:13 AMP).

In Jesus's name! Amen

Dear Father,

I ask for strength today to overcome any obstacles that come my way, whether spiritual, mental, or physical (Revelation 12:11). I trust that Your strength will help me face any challenging circumstance. I ask the Holy Spirit to give me strategies for every area I feel defeated in. Father, guard my heart with Your peace. May my path be directed by Your voice, and I take comfort in knowing You will remain faithful to Your Word and promises as my faith is anchored in You.

In Jesus's name! Amen

Dear Father,

I will allow faith to be my shield as I trust Your plans for my life. I believe every dream, vision, and aspiration I have shall come to pass. As Your word in Habakkuk 2:2 says, write the vision and make it plain. I decree and declare every word You have spoken will begin to manifest in my life, and Your Word will not return void. As your Word says, The Lord does have pleasure in the prosperity of His servants, and Abraham's blessings are mine (Psalms 35:27).

                In Jesus's Name! Amen

Favor

Dear Father,

I pray Your Favor will find me in an uncommon place. I pray Your grace and strength guide me through life as Your rod and staff comfort me. I decree and declare I am no longer waiting on the table to be prepared, but I shall begin to walk in rooms, and the doors of Promises shall open. I decree and declare there shall be no hindrances in this season. Father, I thank You for the joy, love, peace, and faith that will be my portion as purpose brings to overflow in my life. I ask You to perfect everything concerning me, my family, my career, my health, and my finances.

In Jesus's name! Amen

Grief

Dear Father,

Father, I will lift up my eyes to the hill from whence comes my help. My help comes from You (Psalms 121:1-2 NKJV). I ask that You remove the spirit of heaviness from my heart and give me a garment of praise. Father, touch every wound and give me peace that surpasses all understanding as Your rod and staff comfort me. Father, Your Words say, blessed are those who mourn, for they shall be comforted (Matthew 5:4 NKJV). I ask that the Holy Spirit will be my Helper Comforter, Advocate, Intercessor, Counselor, Strengthener, and Standby (John 14:16 AMP).

In Jesus's name ! Amen

Dear Father,

Your word declares You are near to the brokenhearted and save the crushed in spirit (Psalms 34:18). Father, my heart is broken, and I miss my loved ones. The pain is deep in my heart and mind. The grief I am facing weighs heavily on me, and I cannot sleep at night. It has become a burden to my soul. Nevertheless, Your word says, come to me, you all who are heavy laden, and you shall find rest for your souls (Matthew 11:28). Thank You for giving my soul rest.

In Jesus's name! Amen

Health

Dear Father,

Your word is a lamp to my feet and light to my path. Lord, I want my hope, peace, and love to be anchored in You (Psalms 119:105). I plead the blood over my health. I decree and declare sickness will not overtake my body. I decree and declare healing, and wellness shall be my portion. Father, I trust that Your *word will not return to You void concerning me (Isaiah 55:11). For healing is Your children's bread.*

        In Jesus's name! Amen

Dear Father,

I plead the blood against Alzheimer's, dementia, kidney failure, heart failure, any form of organ or bone cancer, pulmonary edema, strokes, heart attacks, diabetes, pulmonary hypertension, and hypertension will not touch my body. My immune system shall function as intended to defend my body from any disease, virus, infection, or bacteria. I plead the blood; I shall not have arthritis, lupus, asthma, liver disease, kidney disease, or any disease that weakens my immune system. My immune system shall function as You created it to stop any disease, virus, infection, or bacteria from harming my body. I shall not die, but live and declare the works of the Lord (Psalms 118:17 NKJV).

In Jesus's name! Amen

Dear Father,

I shall be the lender and not the borrower. I pray that in this season of giving, men and women give into my blossom. Job 22:28 declares, *"If I decree a thing, it shall be established."(NKJV)* I decree and declare that delays, distractions, and lack will not keep me stagnant. I decree and declare open doors, investors, mentorship, fresh business ideas, increased clients, and streams of income. Matthew 7:8 proclaims, "for everyone who asks receives; the one who seeks finds; and to the one who knocks, the door will be opened." (NIV).

In Jesus's name! Amen!

Dear Father,

I decree and declare that the mountains melt like wax before You, Lord (Psalm 97:5). I speak to every mountain that was sent to hinder my progress, and cast it into the sea (Mark 11:22-23). If there is any place I lack faith, I ask that you enlighten the eyes of my understanding so I will know the hope of Your calling (Ephesians 1:17-18). For Jesus is the author and the finisher of my faith (Hebrews 12:2). *I believe You are "able to keep you from stumbling and to present you faultless before the presence of Your Glory with exceeding joy"* (Jude 1:24 NKJV).

In Jesus's name! Amen

Dear Father,

Death and life are in the power of the tongue, and those who love it will eat its fruit." (Proverbs 18:21 NKJV). I tap into Your dunamis power to call things that do not exist as though they did (Romans 4:17). I will bless what God bless and curse what God curse. No weapon formed against me shall prosper (Isaiah 54:17).

In Jesus's name! Amen.

Fear

Dear Father,

You didn't give me the Spirit of fear but power, love, and a sound mind. I decree and declare I walk in power, love, and a sound mind. I will walk boldly in my next as your power builds my courage, strengthens my mind, and opens my heart to Your love. I ask that Your refining fire burn up everything that is not like You and move every doubt in my heart as I walk entirely in my blessings and abundance. *I will not worry about my life, what I will eat or what I will drink; nor about my body, what I will put on* (Matthew 6:25 NKJV). I decree and declare I have no lack, for You shall supply all my needs.

        In Jesus's name! Amen

Dear Father,

I will fear not because I know You are with me. I will not be dismayed, for I know You are my God. Thank You for strengthening, helping, and upholding me with Your righteous right hand (Isaiah 41:10 NKJV). I stand firm in the liberty where Christ has set me free and shall not be entangled with the bondage of fear (Galatians 5:1). I trust Your plan for my life and not my current circumstances. I will not allow anyone to tell me anything different. But I shall be transformed by the renewing of my mind. As I let Your peace rule in my heart and refuse to worry. It is written, *"But those who wait on the Lord shall renew their strength; They shall mount up with wings like eagles, they shall run and not be weary, they shall walk and not faint."* (Isaiah 40:31 NKJV)

In Jesus's name! Amen

Dear Father,

I pray that the weapons of my warfare are not carnal but mighty in God for the pulling down of strongholds, casting down every argument and every high thing that exalts itself against the knowledge of God, and bringing every thought into captivity to the obedience of Christ. I declare and decree I will not fail, I will not give up, I will not give in, I will not die here, I will not lose it all. I shall experience Your fullness and live abundantly in the land of the living. For, the *young lion lacks and suffers hunger, but those that seek the Lord shall not lack any good thing" (Psalms 34:10)*.

In Jesus's name! Amen

Dear Father,

I come before you concerning my family. Father, I ask that there may be *no division in our family but that the members may have the same care for one another (1 Corinthians 12:25 NKJV)*. I pray we have the same mind, heart, and spirit. Father, if there is any place we are divided, unite us that we may have *the same mind and the same judgment(1 Corinthians 1:10)*. As Your word says, for *God is not a God of disorder but of peace—as in all the congregations of the Lord's people (1 Corinthians 14:33 NIV)*.

In Jesus's name! Amen

Dear Father,

I ask You to watch over my family. We believe You are our shepherd, and we shall not want (Psalms 23). We *trust in You and lean not to our own understanding (Proverbs 3:5).* Father, I ask that *You may strengthen each person with might through Your Spirit in their inner man, that Christ may dwell in our hearts through faith, that we will be rooted and grounded in love. (Ephesians 3:17 NKJV).* Thank You for Your *fervent and unfailing love for my family, because love covers a multitude of sins [it overlooks unkindness and unselfishly seeks the best for others]" (1 Peter 4:8).*

In Jesus's name! Amen

Dear Father,

I ask that You heal my parents in every place they are hurting. I pray for You to *restore the years that the locust hath eaten, the cankerworm, the caterpillar, and the palmerworm (Joel 2:25 KJV)*. I ask that every organ, artery, muscle, nerve, blood vessel, joint, and brain function as you created. I plead the blood against Alzheimer's, dementia, kidney failure, heart failure, any form of organ or bone cancer, pulmonary edema, strokes, heart attacks, diabetes, pulmonary hypertension, hypertension, and breast cancers. Father, I ask that You give them a long life. I decree and declare they shall live and not die, but they will declare the works of the Lord (Psalm 118:17).

In Jesus's name! Amen

Dear Father,

I pray for my church family. May You continue to watch over our leaders and keep them protected as Your word, Psalm 105:15, says, *touch not my anoint and do my prophet no harm (NKJV)*. Father, I ask that You continue to give my pastor a heart like Yours *(Jeremiah 3:15)* and teach him how to divide the world rightfully (2 Tim. 2:15). I ask that You continue to enlighten the eyes of their understanding. Father, I ask that as they take care of your house, You will take care of their house. I ask that You restore all they put in the kingdom. I pray no counterattack or retaliation against them shall prosper. Thank you for such a vessel to teach us and help us understand Your plans for my life.

In Jesus's name! Amen

Dear Father,

I come before You to thank You for my spouse. I pray that You will perfect all things that concern them (Psalm 138:8). As they trust in You, lean not to their own understanding but in all their ways acknowledge You, You will direct their path (Proverbs 3: 5-6). May You keep their heart and mind on you because a heart and mind that stays on You will be in perfect peace (Isaiah 26:3). Father, I ask that You fill my spouse with the Fruits of the Spirit, love, joy, peace, forbearance, kindness, goodness, faithfulness, gentleness, and self-control (Galatians 5:22-23). Give them provision for their work and teach them how to rely on You for all their needs, desires, and riches. For You shall supply all their needs according to His riches in glory by Christ Jesus (Philippians 4:19). Lord, I pray You to protect them and let no evil befall them or plague come near their dwelling (Ps.91:10-11). Father, You call us to be helpers to one another and teach us how. (1 Thessalonians 5:11). Lord, teach us how to have compassion for each other even when we don't understand. Teach us to lead and submit according to Your Will (Ephesians 5:22-23). Father, I ask that You lead us by the still waters and green pastures (Psalms 23:3-4) so we may always see life and love in our marriage. Thank You for blessing our covenant.

In Jesus's name! Amen

Dear Father,

I decree and declare (your name and spouse name) is patient and kind; (your name and spouse name) does not envy or boast; (your name and spouse name) is not arrogant or rude (your name and spouse name) does not insist on their own way; (your name and spouse name) are not irritable or resentful; (your name and spouse name) does not rejoice at wrongdoing, but (your name and spouse name) rejoices with the truth (your name and spouse name) bears all things, (your name and spouse name) believes all things, (your name and spouse name) hopes all things (your name and spouse name) endures all things (your name and spouse's name) Love will never end. It is written according to (1 Cor. 13:4-8 ESV)
    In Jesus's name! Amen!

Dear Father,

I ask that you watch over my child(ren) and protect them from harm. I ask that You give Your angels charge over them to keep them in all their ways (Psalms 91:11). May You teach them the way they should go and lead them in the path of righteousness for Your name's sake. Father, I ask that You strengthen their minds to make the right choices and enlighten the eyes of their understanding so they will know the hope of Your calling (Ephesians 1:18). Father, Proverbs 22:6 declares, "train up a child in the way they should go and when they grow older, they will not depart. I ask that my child(ren) be transformed by the renewing of their minds; they may not conform to the patterns of this world (Romans 12:2).

                    In Jesus's name! Amen

Dear Father,

I ask You to strengthen my child(ren)'s mind and heart. May Your peace rule in their heart and mind. Father, I ask You to be their shepherd and lead them in green pastures. I decree and declare that no weapon formed against their mind, heart, destiny, or confidence shall prosper. I bind every mind-binding spirit sent to dethrone their purpose. I ask that You separate them from anyone in their lives who has bad intentions and evil motives as far as the East is from the West(Psalms 103:12). May You give them a spirit of discernment to judge between good and evil.
    In Jesus name! Amen

Dear Father,

I ask that You touch my child(ren) from the crown of their head to the soles of their feet. Father, I ask that no sickness or diseases touch their body and every organ function as You intended. I ask that You place a shield of protection around their brains, heart, and lungs. No cancer, brain disease, heart disease, bone disease, viruses, or any sickness will overtake them. No mental abuse, sexual abuse, mental illness, drugs, gangs, or perversion will overtake them. I plead the blood against premature death; they shall live and declare the works of the Lord (Psalm 118:17) and be steadfast and immovable.

In Jesus's name! Amen

Provider

Dear Father,

Father, I ask that I begin to receive some answers to the prayers and the petitions I have before You. *No matter how many promises You have made, they are "Yes" in Christ (2 Corinthians 1:20 NIV).* I believe You shall supply all my needs according to His riches in glory by Christ. Father, I decree and declare You can do exceedingly abundantly above all I can ask or think, according to the power that works for me (Ephesians 3:20).

In Jesus's name! Amen

Dear Father,

I thank You for being my provider. Thank You for giving me more than just money, peace, strength, and joy. As I go through this season of uncertainty, I will seek Your kingdom and righteousness; all things will be added to me. I stand firm and know that You are with me. Isaiah 41:10 declares, You will strengthen me and uphold me with Your righteous right hand. I will be confident in knowing that if God is for me, who or what can be against me (Romans 8:31 NIV). "For I am persuaded that neither death, nor life, nor angels, nor principalities, nor powers, nor things present, nor things to come, nor height, nor depth, nor any other creature, shall be able to separate me from the love of God, which is in Christ Jesus our Lord (Romans 8:38-39 KJV).

In Jesus's name! Amen

Peace

Dear Father,

Thank You for Your peace that surpasses all understanding. Father, I fellowship with Your peace, not the world's peace. Father, I will allow Your perfect peace to calm me in every situation, knowing You will give me strength and courage for every obstacle. (John 14:27 AMP) I decree and declare I will seek peace and pursue it.

In Jesus name! Amen

Dear Father,

I let the peace of Christ rule in my heart and refused to worry, doubt, or be anxious (Colossians 3:15). Father, Your word says that You will keep those in perfect peace, whose mind is stayed on You because he trusts in You. Father, I believe You are the source of my peace. As it is written, "Great peace have those who love Your law; nothing can make us stumble" (Psalms 119:65).

In Jesus's name! Amen

Dear Father,

Thank You for giving me the gift of the fruits of the spirit. Thank You for giving me peace at all times in every situation. Thank You for being the God of hope and filling me with all joy and peace in believing so that by the power of the Holy Spirit, I may abound in Your hope (Romans 15:13). As it is written, for those who are peacemakers, will plant seeds of peace, and reap a harvest of righteousness (James 3:18 NLT).

    In Jesus's name! Amen

Dear, Father

As I walk into my harvest season, may the words of my mouth and the meditations of my heart be acceptable in Your sight. I pray that the Holy Spirit guides my tongue, for the power of life and death are in it. I ask you, Father, to enlighten the eyes of my understanding and give me a new language to speak to my harvest and any blessings that have been held up. I pray that Your Words of abundance and overflow begin to flow in every area of my life.

In Jesus's name! Amen.

Dear Father,

Let the words of my mouth and the meditation of my heart be acceptable in Your sight both day and night, O Lord, my strength and my redeemer (Psalms 19:14). May my speech be always gracious and seasoned with salt so that I may know how I ought to answer each person (Colossians 4:6). I decree and declare no *corrupt communication shall come out of my mouth, but which is good to the use of edifying, that it may minister grace unto the hearers. And grieve not the holy Spirit of God, whereby ye are sealed unto the day of redemption (Ephesians 4:29-30).*

In Jesus's name! Amen

Anxiety

Dear Father,

I shall not be anxious about anything, but in everything by prayer and supplication with thanksgiving I will make my request be made known to You (Philippians 4:6). Father, for the weapons of my warfare are not carnal but mighty in You for pulling down strongholds, casting down arguments and every high thing that exalts itself against the knowledge of God, bringing every thought into captivity to the obedience of Christ."(2 Corinthians 10:4-5 NKJV) I decree and declare whatever things are true, whatever things are noble, whatever things are just, whatever things are pure, whatever things are lovely, whatever things are of good report, if there is any virtue and if there is anything praiseworthy, I meditate on these things." (Philippians 4:8 NKJV).

In Jesus's name! Amen

Dear Father,

I will cast all my anxieties on You for You care for me (1 Peter 5:7 NIV). I will not be afraid of the terrors by night nor the arrows that fly by day (Psalm 91:5). I believe You are my light and salvation. Whom shall fear? You are the strength of my life. Of Whom shall I be afraid? (Psalms 27:1). Father, I thank You for the thoughts You think towards me. Thank You for the thoughts of peace and not evil, to give me a future and hope (Jeremiah 29:11). I believe in Your plans for my life over anxiety.

    In Jesus's name! Amen

Depression

Dear Father,

Your word in Matthew 11:28 says, come to me all who labor and are heavily laden. Father, I am heavy laden; I come to You for rest. You are near the broken heart and save the crushed in spirit (Psalm 34:18 NKJV). Father, I ask that my heart reflects Your Son's heart, for it is gentle and humble (Matthew 11:29). Thank You for hearing my righteous cry for help and delivering me from all my troubles. I will take Your yoke upon me and learn from You for it is easy, and Your burden is light (Matthew 11:30 NJKV).

In Jesus's name! Amen

Dear Father

I will wait patiently for You, Lord, to hear my cry. I ask that You lift me out of *this slimy pit of the mud and mire. Father, I ask You to set my feet on a rock, give me a place to stand, and put a new song in my mouth* (Psalms 40:1-3 NKJV). I will not stay in this place of no hope. I ask that You give me the garment of praise for the spirit of his heaviness (Isaiah 61:3). I shall be like *a tree planted by the rivers of water that bring forth fruit and its season whose leaf also shall not wither and whatever I do, I shall prosper (Psalms 1:3 NKJV).*

In Jesus's name! Amen

Dear Father,

My spirit is overwhelmed, and my heart is distressed (Psalm 143:4). Answer me speedily: Oh Lord, my spirit fails, do not hide your face from me; lest I be like those who go down into the pit. Father, I desire to hear Your lovingkindness in the morning. I trust You can lift my spirit up to You. Father, I ask that You show me which way I should walk (Psalm 143:8-9). Father, I ask that You revive me, O, Lord, for Your name and righteousness's sake, bring my soul out of trouble (Psalms 143:11).

In Jesus's name! Amen

The Father's Prayer

Our Father,

Hallowed be Your name. Your kingdom come. Your will be done on earth as it is in heaven. Give me this day my daily bread. And forgive my debts, As I forgive my debtors. And do not lead me into temptation, But deliver me from the evil one. For Yours is the kingdom and the power and the Glory forever. Amen."
Matthew 6:9-13 NKJV

Nehemiah's Prayer

"I pray, Lord God of heaven, O great and awesome God, You who keep Your covenant and mercy with those who love You and observe Your commandments, please let Your ear be attentive and Your eyes open, that You may hear the prayer of Your servant which I pray before You now, day and night, for the children of Israel Your servants, and confess the sins of the children of Israel which we have sinned against You. Both my father's house and I have sinned. We have acted very corruptly against You, and have not kept the commandments, the statutes, nor the ordinances which You commanded Your servant Moses. Remember, I pray, the word that You commanded Your servant Moses, saying, 'If you are unfaithful, I will scatter you among the nations; but if you return to Me, and keep My commandments and do them, though some of you were cast out to the farthest part of the heavens, yet I will gather them from there, and bring them to the place which I have chosen as a dwelling for My name.' Now these are Your servants and Your people, whom You have redeemed by Your great power and by Your strong hand. O Lord, I pray, please let Your ear be attentive to the prayer of Your servant, and to the prayer of Your servants who desire to fear Your name; and let Your servant prosper this day, I pray, and grant him mercy in the sight of this man." For I was the king's cupbearer."

Nehemiah 1:5-11 NKJV

Jabez's Prayer

"Father would bless me indeed, and enlarge my territory, that Your hand would be with me, and that You would keep me from evil, that I may not cause pain!"
In Jesus's name! Amen.
(1 Chronicles 4:10 NKJV).

Hannah's Prayer

"My heart rejoices in the Lord; My horn is exalted in the Lord. I smile at my enemies, because I rejoice in Your salvation. "No one is holy like the Lord, For there is none besides You, Nor is there any rock like our God. "Talk no more so very proudly; Let no arrogance come from your mouth, For the Lord is the God of knowledge; and by Him actions are weighed. "The bows of the mighty men are broken, and those who stumbled are girded with strength. Those who were full have hired themselves out for bread, and the hungry have ceased to hunger. Even the barren has borne seven, and she who has many children has become feeble. "The Lord kills and makes alive; He brings down to the grave and brings up. The Lord makes poor and makes rich; He brings low and lifts up. He raises the poor from the dust and lifts the beggar from the ash heap, To set them among princes and make them inherit the throne of glory. "For the pillars of the earth are the Lord's, and He has set the world upon them. He will guard the feet of His saints, but the wicked shall be silent in darkness. "For by strength no man shall prevail. The adversaries of the Lord shall be broken in pieces; From heaven He will thunder against them. The Lord will judge the ends of the earth. "He will give strength to His king, and exalt the horn of His anointed." I Samuel 2:1-10 NKJV

Aaronic Blessing

"The LORD bless me and keep me; the LORD make his face shine on me and be gracious to me; the LORD turn his face toward me and give you peace."
In Jesus's name. Amen
Numbers 6:24-26 NIV

Jermiah's Prayer

"Heal me, O Lord, and I shall be healed; Save me, and I shall be saved, For You are my praise. Indeed they say to me, "Where is the word of the Lord? Let it come now!" As for me, I have not hurried away from being a shepherd who follows You, Nor have I desired the woeful day; You know what came out of my lips; It was right there before You. Do not be a terror to me; You are my hope in the day of doom. Let them be ashamed who persecute me, But do not let me be put to shame; Let them be dismayed, But do not let me be dismayed. Bring on them the day of doom, And destroy them with double destruction!"
In Jesus's name! Amen.

Jeremiah 17:14-18 NKJV

Cover Design: Alvanti Smith
Photos on front cover: Canva

Copyright 2023
Alvanti Smith
All rights reserved.
Printed in the United States of America
Spirit of the Butterfly Publishing

No part of this book may be copied, reprinted, reproduced, or transmitted in any form by any means, electronically, or mechanically without written permission of the author.

Made in the USA
Middletown, DE
16 March 2024